The Youth Athlete Handbook

A Kid's Guide to Being the Ultimate Leader, Competitor, and Teammate

JORDAN BASS, Ph.D.

Copyright © 2021 Jordan Bass, Ph.D.

All rights reserved.

ISBN: 9798546660833

DEDICATION

To my favorite youth sport athletes – Julian and Charlotte

TABLE OF CONTENTS

1	Learning to Love to Compete	Pg. 1
2	Having a Growth Mindset	Pg. 9
3	Making Practice Time Count	Pg. 18
4	Being a Great Teammate	Pg. 25
5	Embracing Your Role on the Team	Pg. 33
6	Taking Feedback from Coaches and Parents	Pg. 40
7	Being a Team Leader On and Off the Field	Pg. 46
8	Developing an Inner Confidence	Pg. 54
9	Bouncing Back from Tough Moments	Pg. 61
10	Enjoying the Journey	Pg. 67

BOOK DESCRIPTION

Are You a Youth Sport Athlete?
If you're reading this book, maybe you just joined your first recreation soccer team. Or, maybe you are nervous about tryouts this weekend for the traveling baseball team you've always dreamed of being on. Whatever your reason or playing level, *The Youth Sports Handbook* will help guide you in your journey as an athlete. Using lessons from your favorite players, you will learn how to "wow" your coaches and be the ultimate leader, competitor, and teammate. What can Olympic Gold Medalist Cat Osterman teach us about bouncing back from a tough loss? How did basketball superstar Kevin Durant lead his teammates to two straight NBA championships? We'll tackle these questions and much more in this fun handbook for athletes seven to 17.

Are You a Youth Sport Parent or Coach?
When I founded my first youth sports club in 2021, I sought out a book to send our U10 baseball players to read before the season that emphasized how to be a leader and good teammate for the upcoming season. I was surprised to find that no such book existed for youth athletes. If you are reading this, you don't need me to tell you how competitive and

structured youth sports have become. In this book, I aim to give your athlete memorable and easy digestible nuggets of advice to help them enjoy their experience and perform their best, no matter the level or age of competition. This book is designed to be read over a week or two by a high school aged athlete, in the month leading up to each season by elementary and middle schoolers, and before bedtime to the newest athletes.

I hope you will enjoy this book and use it improve your youth sports experience as a parent, coach, or player. The chapters can be read out of order as individual lessons, but the book also builds on ideas when read from start to finish. Now, let's get to Chapter One - Learning to Love to Compete!

CHAPTER ONE

LEARNING TO LOVE TO COMPETE

"When you are a competitor and play sports, you're competing every single day!" – Patrick Mahomes, professional football player

In the 2020 Super Bowl, things were not going well for the Kansas City Chiefs. Their opponent was ahead by 10 points with just six minutes left in the biggest game of the season. In the past, many teams had stopped trying as hard and started to accept defeat when they were losing this late in the game. But, the Chiefs were not like those other teams.

They were led by superstar quarterback Patrick Mahomes, a player famous for never giving up and always pushing his team to play hard until the final whistle is blown. With Mahomes pushing his team forward, the Chiefs scored 21 points in a row to become World Champions. After the game, a reporter asked Mahomes how the Chiefs came back to win so quickly. He said, "It's a mindset. **Compete, compete**! That's the biggest thing."

If you have played on a sports team before, you have probably heard your coach or parents tell you that you need to compete or to be a strong competitor. If you watch a sporting event on TV, you will also likely hear the announcer praise a player for being a great competitor or competing hard that day. But, have you ever thought about what it really means to be a good **competitor** or to **compete** during a game or practice? Take a few seconds and think to yourself - what words or pictures come to my mind when you read or hear the word **compete**? I will ask you about these again at the end of the chapter.

As a youth sports coach, the biggest compliment – or nicest thing I can say to a player – is that they are a great competitor. When I was your age all the way until I finished playing in college my favorite thing about sports was competing during practices, games, and even on the playground with my friends.

Competing is by far the thing I miss the most about playing on a sports team.

So, what does it mean to compete or be a competitor? We are not going to try to find a simple definition. Instead, we will talk about some actions that great competitors take every day. Famous athletes have also said many different things about competing that will help guide us. Tennis star Billie Jean King said a competitor was someone who kept trying until they got it right. Baseball manager Joe Torre said competing is about preparation and courage. Hockey legend Wayne Gretzky said that you can't score any goals if you don't take any shots. We'll use each of these to help us learn what it means to be a competitor and how to learn to love to compete.

A competitor is always trying to get better

A player that loves to compete understands that every time they are on the field it is a chance to get better at their sport. They don't waste any practice or game time by goofing off and they always listen to the directions from their coaches. If you love to compete, you understand that you can always improve your skills. This could mean trying to get faster during running drills or throwing a pitch a little bit harder during a scrimmage. Even if you are in the driveway shooting alone, set a goal for what you want to achieve. Is it to make five free throws in a row? Maybe you want to get better dribbling with your left hand. Even if you are just having fun with your friends, have at least one goal in mind every time you play or practice your sport.

A competitor knows there is a difference between competing and winning

You may think that if you win your game or match then you must have competed hard. You may also think that if you lose, then you did not compete hard enough. Neither of these things are always true. Competing hard will help you and your team win, but it does not guarantee you will win. Your competitive focus is on the things you can control – not how well the other team or player performed. If you competed as hard as you could and lost, you should feel good about your effort. If you did not and still won, you should focus on competing harder next time as you may play a better team or person.

A competitor does not get too excited or too upset after a practice or game

The best competitors in the world focus on one play at a time. They are worried about how to make the next shot, throw the next strike, or complete the next pass. They do not get too excited if they hit a home run or too sad if their serve does not go in. Like Billie Jean King said before, a competitor keeps trying until they get it right. Watch a video of your favorite player talking after a big win or loss – you will likely see their focus is on how to use what happened in that game to improve for the next one. When you win, be happy and celebrate with your teammates but make notes on how you can improve. When you lose, be disappointed but support your teammates and do not let it cause you to perform or compete poorly in the next game.

A competitor is not afraid or nervous during big moments. They play for the big moments.

The best competitors understand not everyone is lucky enough to get to play in big moments. It could be the final shot of a big game or hitting a serve on match point in volleyball. Or, like Patrick Mahomes you have the ball with one more chance to score a touchdown. Whatever the "big" moments are in your sport, be competitive and do not be afraid to fail. As Wayne Gretzky said, you miss 100 percent of the shots you do not take. Instead of being nervous or scared, you should feel lucky your coach and teammates trust you enough to be in that position. Competitors play their best when the moments are the biggest and the lights are the brightest. So, when you get your Mahomes Super Bowl moment - be the first person on your team that wants to compete!

Chapter Summary

In this chapter, we learned some of the ways in which you can become a great competitor. Someone who loves to compete is always trying to improve their skills so they can give their team a better chance to win. A competitor also knows that just because you won does not mean you competed your hardest - and you can compete and still lose. Because of this, a competitor does not get too happy or sad after individual games or matches. They use what happened today to help them in future practices and games. Lastly, someone who loves to compete wants to be in big moments. They want the ball when the game is being decided – they want to be the kicker to make the final field goal or the softball hitter at the plate with two outs and the bases loaded.

Now that we have talked about different ways you can be a competitor, what words or images come to mind when you read or hear compete? Hopefully, soon you will have images of yourself competing in your head - – maybe scoring that winning goal! – that you can use to motivate you in the future.

Let's end with one way you can immediately help improve your competitiveness. Women's basketball coach Kara Lawson tells her team to ask themselves after each practice and game – "Did I compete today?" If the answer is no, she says that is okay - as long as it does not happen two days in a row. Take that same idea to your own practices and games. Ask yourself – "Did I compete as hard as I could today?" If the answer is yes - great! If the answer is no, think about why you did not and make it your goal to improve your competitiveness each day.

CHAPTER TWO

HAVING A GROWTH MINDSET

"I can accept failure, everyone fails at something. But I can't accept not trying." - Michael Jordan, former professional basketball player

Michael Jordan is often called the greatest basketball player of all time. When he played with the Chicago Bulls, he won six NBA championships and five Most Valuable Player awards. Jordan is also known to be one of the most competitive athletes in any sport.

Even with all the great things Jordan achieved, he believes his failures helped him succeed as much as his victories. He said, "I've missed more than 9,000 shots in my career. I've lost almost 300 games. I've been trusted to take the game-winning shot 26 times and missed. I've failed over and over and over again in my life. And, that is why I succeed."

If you are like me, you have some days where you struggle on the field or court. Every new shot you try to learn is an airball or every pass you make on the soccer field is stolen. When you have days like this, you have two options. The first option is to be upset, quit, and think "I'll never be able to do this!" The second option is to have what is called a **growth mindset**. If you have a growth mindset, you believe that with hard work and practice you can accomplish the goals you and your coach set for that practice, game, or season.

The opposite of a growth mindset is a fixed mindset – the "I quit!" option above. If you have a fixed mindset, you believe that talent - the skills you are born with - is the only thing that decides how good you will be at sports. A person with a fixed mindset does not practice hard or try new things because they are afraid they will fail. As you can guess, it is very hard to have a fixed mindset and be a successful athlete and teammate.

Instead, we want to approach our sports career with a growth mindset. College teacher Carol Dweck was the first person to come up with this term. She had three rules she gave to United States Olympic coaches to help their athletes perform their best.

Rule #1: In a fixed mindset, try to look talented no matter what. In a growth mindset – learn, learn, learn!

In a fixed mindset, I will only practice the skills I am good at or look good doing. I will be afraid to try new things and will only continue to be good at the same parts of my game. I will not learn anything new because I don't want to suffer any failures. In a growth mindset, I will try to learn something new each practice and push myself to get better – even it means I might look silly in front of my friends and teammates. Let's try an example to show how this rule might look on a competitive softball team.

Jane and Robin both start their first softball season as outfielders. Jane is better at catching flyballs – she is more talented - but has a fixed mindset. During the season, she only really tries during outfield drills at practice because she knows she won't fail and will impress her teammates. She does not try while practicing fielding groundballs because they are harder for her and she is afraid of people thinking she isn't actually that good at softball. She makes a joke every time one goes through her legs and acts like she doesn't care.

Robin has a harder time catching flyballs than Jane – she has less natural talent - but she has a growth mindset. All season, she goes home and asks her parents to throw her more flyballs after practice. The first few weeks at practice the ball bounces off her glove, hits her in the arm, and even falls on her head once! But, none of that stops Robin because she knows if she works hard and practices she will improve. As the season gets closer to the end, Robin starts to catch as many flyballs as Jane. Even better, Robin has also been trying hard while practicing groundballs and has gotten very good at fielding them, too.

So next season, who do you think will have a better chance to start for the team? As you probably guessed, the answer is Robin. She was not afraid to fail, pushed past being scared and looking silly, and learned new skills that will help her during this season and the rest of her softball career.

Rule #2: In a fixed mindset, we don't work too hard or practice too much. In a growth mindset, we work with passion and give a full effort each practice and game.

If I have a fixed mindset, I don't like to show others that I have to work hard to get better or play well – like Jane. I also might tell my friends that "I've always been good" and "I don't have to practice very much." If I have a growth mindset, I work hard each practice and I'm not afraid for my teammates to know that I am working hard, like Robin. I have a passion – or feel very strongly – for the sport I am playing and I know that if I want to be my best self on and off the field it will take a lot of work, and failure, over a long period of time. I will not immediately be great at any skill. The more work I do, the better I will get.

A saying you might hear from your coach is "hard work beats talent when talent doesn't work hard." Take a couple seconds and think about what that saying means to you. If you remember, talent stands for the skills you are born with. To me, that saying means that no matter what skills you have someone will become better than you if you don't continue to work hard and improve.

As a coach, I will always want players that believe in hard work over players that only use their talent. If you were lucky to be born with lots of talent – that's great! If you have a growth mindset, you can now build on that talent and improve even faster by working hard and not being afraid to fail to get better.

Rule #3: In a fixed mindset, when things don't go your way you quit or make excuses. In a growth mindset, you are okay with failing during practice so you know where to improve.

The last rule could be the most important of the three. You may be thinking, why would I ever want to fail? I am really good at dribbling and no one ever steals it from me – do I have to just hand them the ball so I can fail? The answer is no, but remember what we talked about in the first chapter - you shouldn't just compare yourself to the other teams or athletes. Just because you might be the best player in your league right now doesn't mean you always will be, or there isn't a better player you haven't met or played against yet. Set goals for yourself and team and try to meet those no matter who you are playing against that night.

Because if you always succeed, you will not know how to react when you eventually lose and things don't go your way (remember how often the best basketball player ever failed?). In practice, you should get out of your comfort zone so you can improve. Do you never lose the point when you serve in volleyball practice? Try hitting it harder or closer to the line - even it means you hit it out or into the net - so that when the time comes that you need that harder serve you will know you are able to hit it. The failures will let you know where you need to improve so you can get better each practice, game, and season.

Chapter Summary

In the second chapter, we learned all about having a growth mindset. The opposite of a growth mindset is a fixed mindset. In a fixed mindset, I believe that talent is all that matters and I shouldn't practice or work too hard. To be successful at our sport, we should try to have a growth mindset at all times.

If I have a growth mindset, I am not afraid of failure. In fact, failing in practice is the way I will find out what skills I need to spend more time on. Athletes with a growth mindset like to be challenged. They put themselves in new and different situations so when they happen during a game they are ready.

If you are the most talented or the "best" player on your team it is even more important for you to have a growth mindset. You should show your teammates it is okay to fail and the cool thing to do on your team is work hard at practice, no matter how talented you are. If you can get everyone on your team to have a growth mindset, you are ready to have a great season!

CHAPTER THREE

MAKING PRACTICE TIME COUNT

"I am building a fire, and every day I train, I add more fuel. At just the right moment, I light the match." – Mia Hamm, former professional women's soccer player

In 1999, 17-year-old Serena Williams won her first Grand Slam tennis title at the US Open. Over the next twenty years, Serena won 22 more Grand Slam tournaments – breaking the record for most ever. To become the best of all time, Serena had to overcome many obstacles growing up. She did not start playing tennis by taking expensive lessons or joining a private tennis club like many other professional tennis champions. She started practicing on city courts with her Dad as her coach and had to make the most of the available court time. Her family believed in practicing so much that even though Serena was one of the best youth players in the country, she played very few tournaments until she perfected her skills to be good enough to play *professional* tournaments! Later in her career, when she was asked about being lucky Serena said, "Luck has nothing to do with it. I have spent many, many hours - countless hours - on the court working for my one moment in time, not knowing when it would come."

Every athlete loves to play in games. The crowd is cheering, the action is moving fast, and at the end you might get to celebrate a victory. However, some athletes don't love practice. Practice could mean doing the same drills over and over, never getting to keep score to decide who wins, or the worst of all – running to get in better shape! For many people, practice is just the thing you have to do so your coach will let you play in the game that weekend. But as Serena showed us above, you should **view competing in games as your reward for giving your full effort during practice.**

In this chapter, we will focus on ways you can make the most of your practice time. In the two previous chapters, you probably noticed we talked a lot about how being a competitor and having a growth mindset are important while practicing. Using those two ideas as our place to begin, let's discuss some habits you can have to be great at practice.

Come to practice with the same excitement and intensity as games

If you are like my children, you have busy lives. You go to school, do homework, hang out with your friends, and maybe play multiple sports. Your coach probably also has a busy life with their family, work, and coaching your team. All of this means you have a limited amount of time each week to practice your sport and improve your skills. In order to get the most out of a short amount of time, you should come to practice with the same energy and excitement as you do your games.

Don't walk into the gym with your head down already counting down the minutes until you can go home. Instead, treat practice as an opportunity to get better at your sport so you will have a greater chance to celebrate after your next game. In most games, the team that practiced harder is the team that will leave the field victorious.

Treat each drill or training in practice as a mini-competition

In the first chapter, we learned how to love to compete. Now, take that competitive mindset to each part of your practice. You can compete against your teammates, your coach, and even yourself. It could be trying to make 10 shots first in a free throw shooting competition (competing against your teammates), or running fast to beat a time written on the whiteboard (competing against your coach), or swimming a faster lap than you did last practice (competing against yourself).

When you view drills as a competition, you also start to train your mind and body to perform when the pressure is high. If the first time you feel nervous or uncomfortable is during a game, it will be much harder to perform at a high level. Use practice to get used to those feelings so you can "crush it" when they happen during a game.

Set goals and track your progress

You should approach each practice with set goals in your mind. Maybe you know this week you will be working on corner kicks. Before practice, write down your goals for that day. It could be something as simple as I want 75 percent of my attempts to land inside the box. After practice, keep track of how you did and then look back at it before you practice corners the next time. As you continue to work on the same skills, set new goals and follow your progress during the season. Your coaches and parents can be a big help when you are deciding what goals you should try to reach. They can help you make sure the goals are not too easy that they won't challenge you and not too hard that you can't reach them.

For example, now that I am older and slower I love to compete against my friends and myself while playing golf. At the start of each year, I write down my goals and each time I play I update how I'm doing. For example, in 2021 I want to make 100 birdies. So, every time I make one I write down the date and hole where it happened. At the end of the year, I will check to see how I did toward my set goals and how my stats compared to last year. You should keep records and stats like these to help focus your practice time and track how much you have improved each season.

Chapter Summary

You may have heard the old saying that "practice makes perfect." But, my favorite saying about practice is, "If you think practice is boring, try sitting on the bench." If you are not using your practice time to improve your skills, someone else on your team will be more ready to play during game time.

Use the tips in this chapter to improve your practice habits. Bring the same energy and passion to practice that you do to championship games. As we've seen, practice is just as important as those big games. Once you have brought that energy, view every drill as a competition. You can compete against your teammates, coach, or even yourself. Finally, set goals for each practice and keep track of your progress during the season. **You will be amazed how much you improve.**

Go back to the start of the chapter and read the quote from Mia Hamm. She views her game like a fire waiting to be lit. The more fuel, or skills, she can add to it the more impressive and powerful it will be when it's time to perform. Leave this chapter thinking about what fuel you can add to your fire this season.

In the next chapter, we'll dive into how to be a good teammate. You'll see that approaching practice in the ways shown in this chapter is an important part of being a valuable team member. If everyone takes practice seriously and gives their full effort, not only will you benefit but the entire team will get better and hopefully win as many championships as Serena!

CHAPTER FOUR

BEING A GREAT TEAMMATE

"The way a team plays as a whole determines its success. You may have the greatest bunch of individual stars in the world, but if they don't play together, the club won't be worth a dime." – Babe Ruth, former professional baseball player

Misty May-Treanor and Kerri Walsh Jennings were together in a familiar place in the summer of 2012. They were playing for their third straight Olympic gold medal in sand volleyball. The American pair had won in 2004 and 2008 but this year was different. In the final match, they had to play a duo from their own country that was looking to defeat them to become the new best American team. However, Misty and Kerry had a secret weapon on their side – they had been great teammates and played together for over 10 years! They used this to their advantage in winning gold for the third straight Olympics by beating the other American team in straight sets. After the match, Kerri said, "Misty and I have something really special. The world knows it, we know it, and we embrace it. I am so proud to have played the last 12 years with Misty!"

We could spend the entire book discussing how important it is to be a great teammate like Kerri and Misty. If you've played sports before, you know how much time you spend with your teammates both on and off the field. You hang out with them before and after practice, compete side by side during games, and travel together to tournaments. **The enjoyment and success level of a season can often be decided by a simple question: "Is the roster filled with great or bad teammates?"**

When I ask my players what it means to be a great teammate, they usually say things like "making sure everyone is included" or "encouraging someone if they make a mistake." Things like this are definitely important, but being a great teammate goes so much deeper than just being friendly or supportive. Let's talk about a few of my favorite ways to be a great teammate.

A great teammate always gives 100% effort

How hard you practice or play – your effort – is one of the things you can always control on the field. You can't control how good the other team is or if the rain will stop long enough you can play. But, **you can always control your effort** and a great teammate always gives 100 percent.

If you don't give your full effort, it shows disrespect to your teammates and coaches (we'll talk more about respect in a minute). It will also take your coaches attention away from the entire team if they must force you to try hard. A great team is full of players that give maximum effort without having to be told to do so by coaches or parents.

A great teammate holds themselves and their teammates accountable

You should expect a lot out of yourself and your teammates. Holding someone accountable means talking to them if they are not doing what is expected. But, it doesn't mean you just yell at them from across the field. Instead, walk over to your teammate and explain why what they are doing is hurting the team. Here is an example from a youth basketball team.

Miles and James are in the same small group during practice. The team is working in pairs and begins a drill to get more accurate at bounce passes. Miles and his partner are working together well and passing it back and forth without having to chase the ball. But, Miles notices that James and his partner are struggling. Miles stops and watches James bounce it over his partner's head on purpose and start laughing when his partner has to run to go get the ball. What should Miles do?

He has a lot of options for how to react. Miles could simply go back to his own drill and not worry about

James. He could also just go get one of the coaches and tell them James is goofing off and let them take care of it. **But Miles knows that on a great team, the players – not just the coaches - hold each other accountable.** So, he walks over to James and calmly reminds him everyone is trying to get better and if they want to have a successful season, they need to take every part of practice seriously. This is much more powerful than a coach having to correct the behavior. Like Miles, don't be afraid to hold your teammates accountable.

A great teammate has respect for others and understands their actions impact everyone

Once you are on a team, you have a responsibility to respect everyone that helps make your team a success. That means you are kind and helpful to your coaches, your parents, other parents on the team, officials, and fans. Having respect means treating others the way you would want to be treated and doing your part to make the team successful. If you have respect for others, your coach shouldn't have to ask you to help pick up the field after practice and your parents shouldn't have to remind you to bring all the needed equipment to practice or wear the correct jersey to the game.

When you don't do your part, you create more work for someone else and likely harm the team. If you show up late to practice, your partner won't have anyone to warm up with. If you yell at an official and get a technical foul, you've cost your team two points. It is very important to understand that once you join a team, everything you do impacts the other team members. A teammate that has respect for others makes their teammates' and coaches' lives easier – not harder – and doesn't need to be told to do something more than once.

A great teammate is unselfish and understands team success is greater than individual success

A great teammate understands that individual success means nothing if the team is not successful. Hitting a home run when your team is down 12-0 doesn't have close to the same importance as the game winning double in the city championship. **You should always put the team first and do what you can to help everyone on your team succeed.**

Be as happy for team successes as you are for your own. And, when you are struggling don't show negative emotions and bring down your teammates. Always be positive, build up the others around you, and celebrate the successes of others on your team. A game where you score three goals but lose should be less satisfying than scoring a goal and winning.

Chapter Summary

In the fourth chapter, we learned that being a great teammate is more than just being friendly and supportive. Being a great teammate is being unselfish, holding your teammates accountable, and having respect for others. If you are a great teammate, the success of the team means more to us than our individual accomplishments.

Even having one bad teammate around can impact everyone. Use the ideas in this chapter to make sure you are not that bad teammate. If you are already a great teammate, you can use what we talked about so far to help others follow your lead. Don't be afraid to hold others on your team accountable but make sure you are respecting them and your coaches while doing so. Don't yell at or make fun of bad teammates – calmly and directly explain how their actions negatively impact everyone and will hurt your chances for a successful year. If you hold everyone accountable, hopefully in a few months you'll be surrounded by a group that is full of great teammates!

CHAPTER FIVE

EMBRACING YOUR ROLE ON THE TEAM

"Everyone on your team is important. Importance knows no rank." – Coach K, college men's basketball coach

Even if you are not a basketball fan, I'm guessing you've heard of LeBron James, Michael Jordan, and Kobe Bryant. However, none of them hold the record for most NBA championships in modern basketball. That honor belongs to Robert Horry, a player that only scored an average of seven points a game during his career but played a key role in seven NBA titles. Every year, Horry would embrace his role as a three-point shooter when the game was on the line. His habit of making important shots earned him the nickname "Big Shot Bob" and helped him earn over 50 million dollars during his 16-year career in the NBA.

Every athlete grows up dreaming of being the star player on their team. Thoughts of hitting ace serves or scoring goals have likely motivated you to practice and improve your skills. But, not everyone can be the star player for their team. **In fact, the best teams are full of players that understand their roles.** As Coach K said above, every role on the team is important. Pat Riley, another basketball coaching legend, said "the key to teamwork is to learn a role, accept that role, and strive to become excellent playing it."

A role can be defined simply as the responsibility each player has for the team to be successful. Your coach and parents will work with you to define your role on the team for that season. Let's look at an example of what roles might exist on a youth baseball or softball team.

Starting Pitchers - Your team will have at least a couple players that will be expected to pitch multiple innings when they are in the game. A starting pitcher should throw strikes, pitch to contact, and eat up innings for their team.

Relief Pitchers – When a starting pitcher gets tired, hits their pitch limit, or struggles you will need pitchers that are ready to come in. Relief pitchers will need to learn to pitch with runners on base and be able to warm up their arms quickly.

Aggressive Hitters – Your team will have a couple hitters who focus on trying to get extra base hits, drive in their teammates, and hit for power. They are okay with striking out sometimes so they can continue to be aggressive and create runs for the team.

Patient Hitters - These hitters will be more patient, take more pitches, and hit for contact. They will try to not strikeout and put the ball in play while tiring out the pitcher.

Pinch Hitters – It's likely you'll have players that will not start the game. Their role is to support their teammates when they are not playing while also being ready to come in when asked by their coach. They will need to learn how to be both an aggressive and patient hitter so they can be used in any situation.

Defense and Speed Focused Players – Every team should have players that can steal a base or put pressure on the defense with their speed. Your team should also have athletes that are great on defense to help a team hold a lead in the last innings of a game.

No matter what team you are on, there will be multiples roles that need to be filled. Like Robert Horry, **even the smallest of roles can be the difference between first and second place.** There are a couple ways you can help yourself and your teammates embrace their roles this season.

Study professional athletes that have been successful in your role

You can learn a lot by seeing how the best players in the world embrace their roles. Some of the most famous pitchers in Major League Baseball only expect to pitch one inning each night. How do they prepare? What skills do they work on that are specific to their role? What things do they do that makes them successful? These are all questions that will help you improve in your role.

Understand no role is too small and each role is important to the success of the team

My favorite players I have coached understood that **for our team to be successful, everyone has to believe in what we are doing.** Each player must embrace their role and believe that without them, our team could not be successful. A role as simple as "bringing positive energy to the team" can be the difference between a win or loss at the end of a tournament when everyone is tired.

Be curious and ask your coach – "How can I help the team?"

Your coach should know what skills you have and the ways you can help the team win. But, you can always ask what they expect out of you and how you can improve and grow your role on the team. Your coach will appreciate you wanting to improve and can make it clear what they expect from you each game. Don't be afraid to ask for a bigger role – as long as you are willing to work to earn that role.

Don't try to do everything - take pride being the best player at your role

Don't waste time and energy comparing yourself to others with a different role. Focus on being the best person at your role on your team, in your league, or in your city. You will be a favorite of your coaches and teammates if they can rely on you to fulfill your role each game.

Chapter Summary

The best teams in history were full of players that understood and accepted their roles. A successful basketball team needs players focused on rebounding as much as they need scorers. **One player not performing in their role, no matter how big or small, is often the difference between being happy or disappointed after a close match.**

A good way to learn what is important in your role is to study professional athletes in the same position as you. Does your coach rely on you to come in and rush the quarterback on third down? Find out who is the best at that in the NFL and read and watch everything you can on what makes them successful.

You should also support your teammates and encourage them when they perform well in their role. Don't just cheer when a teammate scores a goal – show the same excitement for a tackle that stops a breakaway. Lastly, talk to your coach about how you can improve in your role and ways you could build on your skills to take on a bigger role this season or in future years.

CHAPTER SIX

TAKING FEEDBACK FROM COACHES AND PARENTS

"A good coach will make players see what they can be rather than what they are." – Ara Parseghian, former Notre Dame head football coach

The Seattle Seahawks could taste it. They were one yard from the end zone with just 26 seconds left in the 2015 Super Bowl. A touchdown and they would be champions for the second straight season. They ran a quick pass play expecting to catch their opponent – the New England Patriots – in a run stopping defense.

However, Patriots defender Malcolm Butler knew when the Seahawks came out in that formation they might be passing. His instincts were correct and he jumped in front of the receiver for an interception to win the Super Bowl for the Patriots. After the game, Butler credited his coach for correcting him when they practiced that play so he was ready for the biggest moment of his life.

We've all been there. It feels like you can't do anything right on the field and your coach is constantly correcting you. You may be thinking "why is Coach picking on me" or "why doesn't Coach like me?" It is natural to feel this way, but usually what is happening is the opposite of what you are feeling. It isn't that the coach doesn't like you or is picking on you – it is that they care deeply about your success and want to help you improve on and off the field.

The same is likely true for your parents and family members. When they give you feedback, they aren't trying to make you feel bad or get upset on the court. They just want the best for you and to see you experience the joy that comes from being successful. As the quote at the start of the chapter shows, a good coach helps players become better than even the player believed they could be. The ability to take feedback is called **being coachable**. We're going to discuss a couple ways you can become more coachable this season.

Be an active and engaged listener

When your coach is talking to you, make eye contact and nod your head when they make important points or ask if you understand. You should show your coach you are engaged with what they are saying and are listening to their feedback. Coaches do not like to repeat themselves and being an active listener will help you understand what they are saying the first time. Doing this will also save time during practice.

Respond to the message, not the tone of voice

Your coach has a busy job during practices and games. They have lots of different tasks, many that have to be completed at the same time for a team to be successful. So, sometimes they may have to tell you something quickly in a tone of voice that doesn't sound very friendly. This isn't because they don't care or are upset with you, it is because they need to move on to the next play or situation. React to what they say, not how they say it.

If you don't understand, don't be afraid to ask

If something your coach says is confusing, or you aren't sure what to do on a certain play you should always ask for help. Coaches make mistakes, too, and asking follow-up questions is always a good idea. Your coach would rather you be 100 percent sure of what they meant than be afraid to ask for more information. If you're an active and engaged listener, you'll also be sure you aren't asking about something that the coach already discussed.

Don't be too cool to take feedback, the best athletes in world rely on coaches for help

There is no honor or glory in going at it alone in sports. At the highest professional level, a coach plays a vital role in helping athletes improve and making teams successful. The same is true in youth sports. Asking for help or getting advice from a coach doesn't mean you are weak or not as good as someone else. **You should want as much information and help as possible to make you the best player and person you can be in and outside of sports.**

Pass the feedback onto members of your team

In the next chapter, we'll discuss how to be a leader on your team. One way is to use the feedback given to you by coaches to help other members of your team. For example, if your coach tells you they want the midfielders to play closer to the goal remind your teammates to move up when they drift downfield. Your coach will appreciate the help and as we talked about earlier, messages from teammates can carry a bigger impact than those from a coach.

Chapter Summary

In this chapter, we discussed how to be coachable. Taking feedback is an important part of sports and even the best players in the world need outside help. Make sure you are an active and engaged listener when your coach is talking to you or the whole team. And, don't be too cool to take feedback from your coaches.

If your coach isn't giving you any feedback, that is when you should start to worry. If you aren't open to taking feedback, your coach may simply stop trying to help you. If you go a couple practices and your coach doesn't give you advice, it may mean you are not being coachable. If this happens, ask your coach what you can do to improve and then use the techniques above to be sure you are being coachable.

CHAPTER SEVEN

BEING A TEAM LEADER ON AND OFF THE FIELD

"Putting yourself out there is hard, but it's so worth it. I don't think anyone who has ever spoken out, or stood up or had a brave moment, has regretted it. It's empowering and confidence-building and inspiring. Not only to other people, but to yourself." – Megan Rapinoe, professional soccer player

At the beginning of the 2018 NBA playoffs, the Golden State Warriors were under a lot of pressure. The year before, they won the NBA title by building a "super team" with Kevin Durant, Steph Curry, and Klay Thompson. To start the 2018 playoffs Steph Curry, the longtime leader of the Warriors, was injured and they were facing the always tough San Antonio Spurs after ending the season losing 10 of their last 17 games. It was time for a new leader to appear – and that player was Kevin Durant.

Reporters asked Durant if he was ready to take on a leadership role. He responded, "I'm a leader in the things that matter. I don't really care about perception anymore when it comes to my game. I'm about showing my teammates what I can do, working every single day and trying to be the hardest worker when I step on the court. That shows and means more than me coming out and saying, 'I'm the leader.''

Durant led the Warriors to a 4-0 sweep of the Spurs in the first round and onto their second straight NBA title with a win over LeBron James. Durant was also named the Finals MVP for the second straight season. One of his teammates said Durant "holds guys accountable. When you see a guy like that, first in the gym and last to leave, he's always getting better and supporting his teammates. There's no better leader. That's what makes him so great."

As Megan Rapinoe and Kevin Durant described above, being a leader is both the hardest and most rewarding thing you can do as a member of a sports team. **Being a leader isn't something you only do for a couple days, or something you can turn off when you're not feeling it.** But, a team needs leaders – strong and consistent leaders – to reach greatness. We're going to spend the rest of this chapter discussing the traits and actions of great leaders that you can use to take on this role on your team.

A great leader is an extension of the coaches

As we have discussed earlier, players are more likely to listen to feedback from their teammates than they are from their coaches. A team leader needs to understand what their coaches expect and can reinforce those messages. Leaders should meet individually with coaches, share their feedback on the team, and understand what the coach needs from the leader for the team to be successful.

A great leader sets a high standard and holds people accountable

In Chapter Four, we learned about Miles and James on a basketball team. In that story, Miles holds James accountable for not trying hard in practice. In the beginning of the season, leaders may have to do something like that every practice until the team understands what is expected. However, in order to hold people accountable, the leader has to be the hardest worker. **They cannot expect others to do things they won't do themselves.** Being a leader doesn't mean you don't have to help shag balls after hitting practice – it means you should be the first to grab a ball.

A great leader has a relationship with everyone on the team

If you want to be a leader, you must learn about all the members of your team. You don't have to be friends with each player – although it helps – but you do need an understanding of what motivates each of the team members. How do they respond when you give them feedback? Do they like it when you do it in front of the team or would they rather you tell them one-on-one? What are their hobbies outside of the team? What are some non-sports things you can talk to them about? These are just a few of the questions you should be able to answer about everybody on your squad if you are a leader.

A great leader shows empathy and puts the needs of others first

If you want to be a great leader, you cannot be selfish or care about yourself over the success of the team. You also must show empathy – or understand the emotions of others. **It is important to realize how others feel and do everything in your power to improve their experience on the team.** If you are a great leader, you will need to take time away from improving your own skills to help others, both physically and emotionally.

A great leader is also a great communicator

In order to lead your team, you must be able to communicate effectively with the players and coaches. You should think before you speak, understand that everyone may respond differently to what you say, and be willing to take the time to make sure your messages are understood. You should be comfortable with speaking in front of people and having tough conversations. Great ideas are lost if the leader can't communicate them.

A great leader has both confidence and courage

If you don't believe in yourself (confidence) or aren't willing to make tough decisions (courage), you won't be as successful as you could be as a leader. Showing confidence both in yourself and the team will help your team members follow you. Leaders will also have to be involved in tough situations – asking players on their team to work harder, standing up for a teammate that was harmed by another team, and solving disagreements between teammates are all examples of a leader showing courage.

A great leader is deeply competitive

In the first chapter, we learned how to love to compete. The leaders on your team should also be the most competitive players. They should care the most about winning, improving, and making progress as a team. A leader hurts the most when the team performs poorly and feels the most pride when a team accomplishes something great. This deep competitive feeling will also rub off on other team members that respect their leaders.

Chapter Summary

Being a leader is hard work. It requires dedication, sacrifice, confidence, and empathy. But, **being a leader is also the most rewarding position you can hold on a team.** It will allow you to be involved with every aspect of the team and also prepares you for leadership positions in the future.

To lead, you need to have a relationship with everyone on the team. You should understand the best way to communicate with each team member and be an extension of your coaches. You also must set a high standard for yourself and others and be comfortable talking to teammates that do not meet those standards. This will sometimes cause teammates to be upset with you - this is something you will have to get used to.

Lastly, being a leader is not a temporary position. You have to be committed to leading, and you can't take days off from the role. This may sound intimidating, but as a leader you can have a huge impact on your team and your teammates.

CHAPTER EIGHT

DEVELOPING AN INNER CONFIDENCE

"Anytime you go up against the best and you succeed — you prove yourself — you're just putting money in your confidence bank. It's a memory you have, that you were successful. You just carry that with you." – Sue Bird, professional basketball player

In 2003, Annika Sorenstam was clearly the best golfer on the LPGA Tour. That season, she won her sixth Player of the Year award and captured two major championships to complete the career Grand Slam. However, the thing she will likely be most remembered for in 2003 is playing a tournament on the men's PGA Tour. Sorenstam was invited to play at a tournament in Texas, becoming the first woman to play on the PGA Tour in close to 50 years. She led the tournament in driving accuracy and finished ahead of 15 PGA players on the leaderboard. Eighteen years later, Sorenstam is still winning major tournaments – most recently the U.S. Senior Women's Open by eight shots in 2021.

Sorenstam credits her inner confidence for her long and successful professional career. "My mental strength was probably my 15th club." Sorenstam said. "I was able to stay positive, forget about bad shots, stay in the moment, and trust myself. A lot of people have doubts in their minds and when you have doubts there is tension, and hesitation, and you don't perform."

Of all the skills we have talked about in this book, confidence is the toughest to teach. This may be because confidence usually comes as a result of all the things we have talked about in the first seven chapters. For example, if I make my practice time count I'll be more confident when the game is on the line because I know my skills have improved. If I love to compete, I'll be more confident during difficult situations because I know how to handle the pressure. If you work on the skills we've discussed so far, your confidence will naturally increase. Below are some more tips for increasing your confidence.

Practice positive self-talk and convince your mind you can be the best at your role

Draymond Green is often said to be the most confident professional basketball player in the NBA. Even though he is not near the most skilled player in the league, he has played a key role on multiple championship teams because of his basketball smarts and defensive ability. When asked by a reporter why he believed he was the best defender ever, Draymond said "If you're trying to do something meaningful and you don't have the mindset that you are the best ever then you've failed already. And that has been my mindset since I can remember. That will be my mindset as long as I can remember anything—that I am the best ever at what I do. And every day that I step on the basketball floor I will strive to be that."

We should all take Draymond's mindset and apply it to our lives. Positive self-belief will help you get through tough situations and allow you to thrive when the competition is the highest. If you ever feel doubt, make yourself believe you are the best because you've done the work to succeed in this situation. But, this only works if you actually prepare to be the best at your role. Annika and Draymond both worked for thousands of hours at their sport so they can convince their mind they are the best. Put in the work so you can do the same. You can also develop a mantra that you repeat to yourself when you start to feel nervous – find a phrase that relaxes you and repeat it in your mind when the time is right.

Let go of your fear, embrace the moment

Sports are fun! Or, at least they should be fun. If you're reading this book, it means you are so lucky that you get to play youth sports. Someone has taken the time to sign you up, pay for your fees and equipment, and find a coach and team for you to play for this season. Feel happy about the chance to play

– don't be afraid you might lose or make a bad play. Be confident that you have done the work to be good at your sport and don't let the fear of failing even enter your mind. Let all the things you worked on in practice, the hours you spent in the gym improving, and the gratefulness you have to play a sport for fun push fear out of your thoughts.

Focus on yourself and your team, don't worry about things you can't control

One of my favorite sayings is that "comparison is the thief of joy." For us, that means comparing ourselves to others can take away our feelings of happiness. You can't control if the players on the other team are taller than you, older than you, or throw faster than you. So, if we can't change any of that why would we even worry about them? The answer is, we shouldn't.

Focus on yourself, your teammates, and how hard you have worked to get to this moment. Know in your mind that you've done everything you can to succeed, and you are ready to perform. Even if you miss five three pointers in a row, you should have the confidence to know you will make the next one because you prepared for this moment. That is all you can control, and thus all you should worry about.

"Be curious, not judgmental." – Walt Whitman

If you want to improve your confidence, you should always be curious. Curious of how you could be a better player, better teammate, and team member. Study the game, study the best players in the game, and use what you find to improve. There is no need to judge anyone for what they do or how they play – remember we can't control that. If you find yourself starting to judge others, it's probably because you are feeling insecure. Maybe you haven't worked as hard as you could this week in practice or you've been a poor teammate lately. When you start to feel this way, figure out why as soon as possible and change it so you can move back from judgmental to curious.

Chapter Summary

Developing an inner confidence is very important to being a successful athlete. It is difficult to be successful in sports if you don't believe in yourself. In this chapter, we learned a few tips that will help improve your confidence. First, you will become more confident the harder you work and the more prepared you feel for the big moments.

You should also always practice positive self-talk and convince your mind that you are the best in your role. Maybe that means you are the best defender like Draymond Green or most accurate driver like Annika Sorenstam. Whatever your role is on your team, put in the work and then remind yourself that you are the best when you get nervous or insecure.

It also isn't important what players on the other team are doing – you shouldn't waste your time comparing yourself or your team to them. We only want to worry about the things we can control. Don't get intimated or overconfident based on what the opponent is doing each game. Instead, focus on what you need to be doing to succeed that night. But more than anything, believe in yourself and don't let fear creep into your mind. You're playing a game for fun, embrace that opportunity and enjoy the moment knowing you are prepared to shine.

CHAPTER NINE

BOUNCING BACK FROM TOUGH MOMENTS

"You're not going to win every game. You're not going to win every pitch. You're not going to win every at bat and you're going to have to figure out how you're going to bounce back."
- Cat Osterman, professional softball player

Jordan Larson had achieved success at every level as a volleyball player. She was a standout high school player in small town Nebraska, she won a national championship at the University of Nebraska, and she had won multiple league championships as a professional. But, in her two Olympics appearances with the American team she had fallen short of a gold medal – winning silver and bronze. In the 2020 Olympics, Larson had her last shot to win the gold.

Before the semifinal match, Larson said "If we've done everything and come up short, I'll be okay with that. In the last Olympics, we took the bronze, but I thought we gave everything we had, and that's what we walked away with. I want the most out of this team, and if that means walking away with gold, that's fantastic. But life is going to go on." Larson went on to lead the American team to their first gold medal without losing a set and she was able to score the final point for the USA.

No matter how hard we train, how confident we are, and how much we feel like we deserve to win sometimes the game is not going to go our way. There is a saying, "that is why they play the game" to show that you can't always predict who is going to win or lose. But as we have discussed in this book, you can learn so much from a loss and turn it into a long term positive. Let's discuss a few strategies for bouncing back from tough moments.

Use the feelings that come from a loss as motivation in the next practice

If you are a competitive person, losing is one of the worst feelings. It is a combination of a bunch of bad feelings – disappointment, sadness, regret, and sometimes anger. It's okay to be upset after a loss – that means you have learned to love to compete and you are invested in the success of the team.

But resist the urge to feel sorry for yourself. Don't complain, make excuses, or say the game was unfair. Instead, make a mental note about what you are feeling then the next time you don't want to train or need a little extra motivation at practice remember those feelings.

Don't let one bad result lead to another loss

In a popular television show, the coach tells his team to be like a goldfish after a bad performance. He said a goldfish only can remember things for ten seconds before they forget and that is how he wants the team to be with the game. For us, that means don't let one loss or bad game impact your confidence. Just because you missed a couple shots today doesn't mean you will in the next game – unless you start to believe that is true.

We all have poor performances and regrets – but the best players use those as a reason to train harder and improve their skills while still remaining confident. If we win every game easily, we won't know what we need to be better at for the next game or next season. Use losses to help you improve for the next game and don't let them impact your confidence or cause you to not try as hard next time.

Don't be afraid to ask for help if you are struggling on or off the field

If you have a tough season or a tough year, you shouldn't go through it alone. **Be open and ask your family, coaches, and teammates for help.** As we talked about earlier, even the best players ever need help to be successful. No one is expecting you to get better at hitting a fastball by yourself – the reason we join a team is so we can go through the good and bad things together. If you are having trouble being confident, tell your coach, teacher, or family member how you are feeling and they will likely know ways to help. Sports and life are more enjoyable when we experience them with others.

Chapter Summary

This chapter was all about how to bounce back from tough moments. We learned to use the feeling of losing to motivate us the next time we might not be feeling it at practice. We also learned that one bad performance shouldn't impact your confidence. If you remember earlier in the book, Michael Jordan talked about how many shots he had missed, games he had lost, and how those helped him get better.

More importantly, you shouldn't feel like you have to go on this sports journey alone. Teammates, coaches, and family members are here to celebrate your successes with and be there to help you get through tough moments on and off the court.

CHAPTER TEN

ENJOYING THE JOURNEY

"Let me win. But if I cannot win, let me be brave in the attempt." – Special Olympics oath

If you have made it this far in the book, I hope you've learned a few skills and ideas that will help you in your journey as an athlete. But, **I also want to make sure you enjoy that journey.** When you are older like me, you will miss being on the field or court every weekend with your buddies. The feeling of a game winning shot or representing your town is not something you will likely get to have as an adult. So, enjoy it while you can! We'll end this book with a few quick tips to enjoy your time as a youth sport athlete.

Don't have any regrets at the end of the season

At the end of your season, I want you to be able to say that you did everything you could to be successful. I don't want you to have to look back and wish you would have tried a little harder, listened to your coach more, or had a better relationship with your teammates. Use the skills we've talked about in this book to maximize your experience so you don't leave the season wishing you had done things differently.

Only worry about your own expectations

You should set your own goals and expectations at the beginning of the season. As we talked about, your family members or coaches can help you with this but they are eventually yours to accomplish. Focus on achieving your own goals and don't worry about what other people think you should do. They aren't the person playing your role – you are – so you should only be concerned with meeting your own expectations. Be honest with yourself and confident in your abilities when setting goals.

Focus on the process, not the results

In the years after your season, you won't remember each game you lost or the practices that were really hard. But, you will remember the friendships you developed with your coaches and teammates, the big moments and wins your team had, and the fun times you had on and off the field. Make sure you enjoy those moments when they happen and don't let a loss ruin your entire experience with your team.

Chapter Summary

Thank you for taking the time to read this book! I hope you will use the ideas discussed in each chapter to improve your experience. Being a youth sports athlete is a very exciting time and I'm jealous you are going through it right now. I hope you have a great season with your team and continue to love to compete as you get older and move on in your youth sports career!

ABOUT THE AUTHOR

Jordan Bass, Ph.D. is a university professor, middle school athletics director, former collegiate athlete, author, and youth sports club founder. After a very average tennis career, Jordan completed his Ph.D. in Sport Management at Florida State University and is currently the Director of the highly ranked Sport Management program and Amateur Sport Research Center at the University of Kansas. He has published over 50 academic articles, three textbooks, serves as the Athletics Director at Saint John Catholic School, and founded the Lawrence Meadowlarks youth sports club in 2021. He lives in Lawrence, Kansas with his wife Robin and two favorite youth sport athletes/children, Julian and Charlotte.

Made in the USA
Coppell, TX
30 August 2025

54068390R00046